This book belongs to:

....

Using This Book

- Use the scenarios in this book as starting points for discussions with your child. Ask them to find the picture stickers and answer the questions.

- Use the gold star stickers to praise their successes, and to encourage their healthy eating habits.

- Fill in the 'I will' tasks on the wipe-clean reward chart, and the star targets and rewards. Your child will enjoy joining in with this too, particularly in choosing the rewards. They will love the sense of responsibility, and the excitement of working towards the treats they've chosen.

- Rewards need not be big, but they should be meaningful to your child: an extra bedtime story, baking a cake, going to the swimming pool or the park, having a friend to play, a pocket money treat – something that they enjoy, and that you feel is appropriate for what they have achieved.

- Always keep a positive attitude and focus on their achievements. Never deny a reward that has been agreed and earned.

- Your child will soon appreciate that healthy eating can be fun, and these positive early habits will help to encourage good health and nutrition throughout their lives.

About the Author

Jo Stimpson is a qualified nutritionist and expert author with over 25 years' experience working in food, health and nutrition. Tackling issues including weight management, childhood obesity and digestive health, Jo has a passion for her profession and for improving lives through better nutrition.

ISBN 978-1-78270-211-5

Copyright © Award Publications Limited

All rights reserved. No part of this publication may be reproduced or utilised in any form or by any means electronic or mechanical, including photocopying, recording, or by any information storage and retrieval system now known or hereafter invented, without the prior written permission of the publisher.

This edition first published 2025

Published by Award Publications Limited,
The Old Riding School, Welbeck, Worksop, S80 3LR

/awardpublications   @award.books   @award_books
www.awardpublications.co.uk

Printed in China

The Children's Book of HEALTHY EATING

Jo Stimpson

Illustrated by Helen Stanton

award

You Are What You Eat

Food and drinks are our fuel. They provide our bodies with energy and help us grow. Certain foods help us fight off illnesses, while others help us build strong bones and teeth. Eating the right balance of foods is important so that our bodies can work properly.

Getting the Right Balance

Foods are grouped together according to the nutrition they provide. Eating a wide variety of foods from each food group will make sure you have a healthy, balanced diet. Try to eat at least 5 handfuls of fruit and vegetables a day, and include plenty of starchy foods so you have energy for school and playing with your friends.

No Time for Breakfast

Liam gets up late this morning and doesn't have time for breakfast. At school he is tired, hungry and grumpy and doesn't feel like playing with his friends.

Why should you eat breakfast?

Good Start to the Day

Liam goes to bed early and sets his alarm for the morning so that he has time for breakfast. He has eggs on toast and a glass of orange juice. This gives him plenty of energy to play and for his lessons.

Can you think of a healthy breakfast?

I eat a healthy breakfast

Getting a Tummy Ache

Molly doesn't like vegetables. She often has tummy ache and has problems going to the toilet. The school nurse suggests that she finds a few fruits and vegetables that she likes.

What happens if you don't eat fruit or vegetables?

5-a-day Keeps Tummy Aches Away

Dad takes Molly to the market to look for some fruits and vegetables that she likes. She discovers some that are really tasty. Now she eats these with her meals and soon her tummy starts to feel better. **What are your favourite vegetables?**

I like to try new fruit and vegetables

Not Drinking Enough

Rasheed always forgets to drink enough water. He sometimes feels dizzy and tired, or has a headache, so can't concentrate on his schoolwork.

How might you feel if you don't drink enough?

Drinking Plenty of Water

Rasheed takes a water bottle to school and puts it on his desk to remind himself to drink. He fills it up at break time too. He feels more alert and gets his best score in maths.

I drink at least 6–8 cups of water a day

How can you make sure you drink enough?

Eating Sweets for Energy

Isla would like to do sport, but never has enough energy. She thinks that eating sweets will give her the energy she needs, but the boost they give her doesn't last very long and soon she feels hungry again. **Why shouldn't you eat sweets to give you energy?**

Eating Starchy Foods for Energy

Isla's PE teacher suggests she eats starchy foods, such as pasta, rice and potatoes, that will give her energy for longer. Isla has noodles at lunchtime and doesn't feel tired or hungry in class that afternoon.

How many starchy foods did you eat today?

Can't Eat Dairy Foods

Joshua has a lactose intolerance, which means he feels poorly if he drinks milk or foods that are made with milk. But he needs 2–3 portions of calcium-rich foods a day to keep his bones and teeth healthy. **What can happen to people who have food intolerances?**

Substituting Dairy Foods

The doctor tells him he should drink dairy-free milk and eat lactose-free cheeses instead, as these contain calcium. These 'substitute' foods will give him the calcium he needs.

How can people with food intolerances get all the nutrients they need?

I keep my bones healthy

Not Enough Protein

Lara visits the school nurse because she feels tired all the time. The nurse asks her if she eats foods such as meat, fish, eggs, beans or lentils. These foods give us both protein and an important nutrient called iron. **Why is it important to eat protein-rich foods?**

Eating Protein Foods

Lara starts to eat more protein and iron-rich foods and soon has more energy to play with her friends. This makes her feel much happier and healthier.

Can you name a food you eat that contains iron?

Eating Too Much

Ben enjoys his food and always has lots on his plate. He thinks this will give him lots of energy to play football, but he finds he feels heavier and is slower at running for the ball.

Why shouldn't you eat more than you need?

Eating the Right Amount

Ben's mum suggests that he has smaller plates of food. After a few weeks he feels lighter and faster and is able to help his team score more goals.

How do you know if you have eaten enough food?

Eating Alone

Kyle doesn't like sitting next to his friend Grace at lunch because she has bad table manners. Grace is sad that no one wants to sit with her, so Kyle decides to explain politely to her why.

Why should we have good table manners?

Eating with Friends

Grace becomes more considerate and improves her table manners. Soon all her friends come and join her at the table. Grace is happier and enjoys her food more when she eats with her friends.
How can you improve your table manners?

Eating Out Often

The Jackson family like to eat out regularly. This often means eating junk food and drinking fizzy drinks. They all feel tired and sluggish.

Why should eating out be a treat rather than something you do all the time?

Cooking at Home

Aiden suggests cooking at home instead. The children help with the cooking and everyone has lots of fun. Eating a healthy, fresh, home-cooked meal together helps them feel much better too.
What could you cook with your family?

Not Eating Regularly

At school Daisy and her friend Olivia don't eat much at lunchtime because they are too busy talking. They are so hungry after school that they eat lots of unhealthy snacks very quickly. They feel a bit sick.
What happens if you don't eat your lunch?

Eating Regularly

The next day Olivia eats all of her lunch and has a healthy snack at home after school. Eating three meals and two healthy snacks a day keeps you feeling much healthier.

Can you think of a healthy snack?

I eat my lunch

Toothache

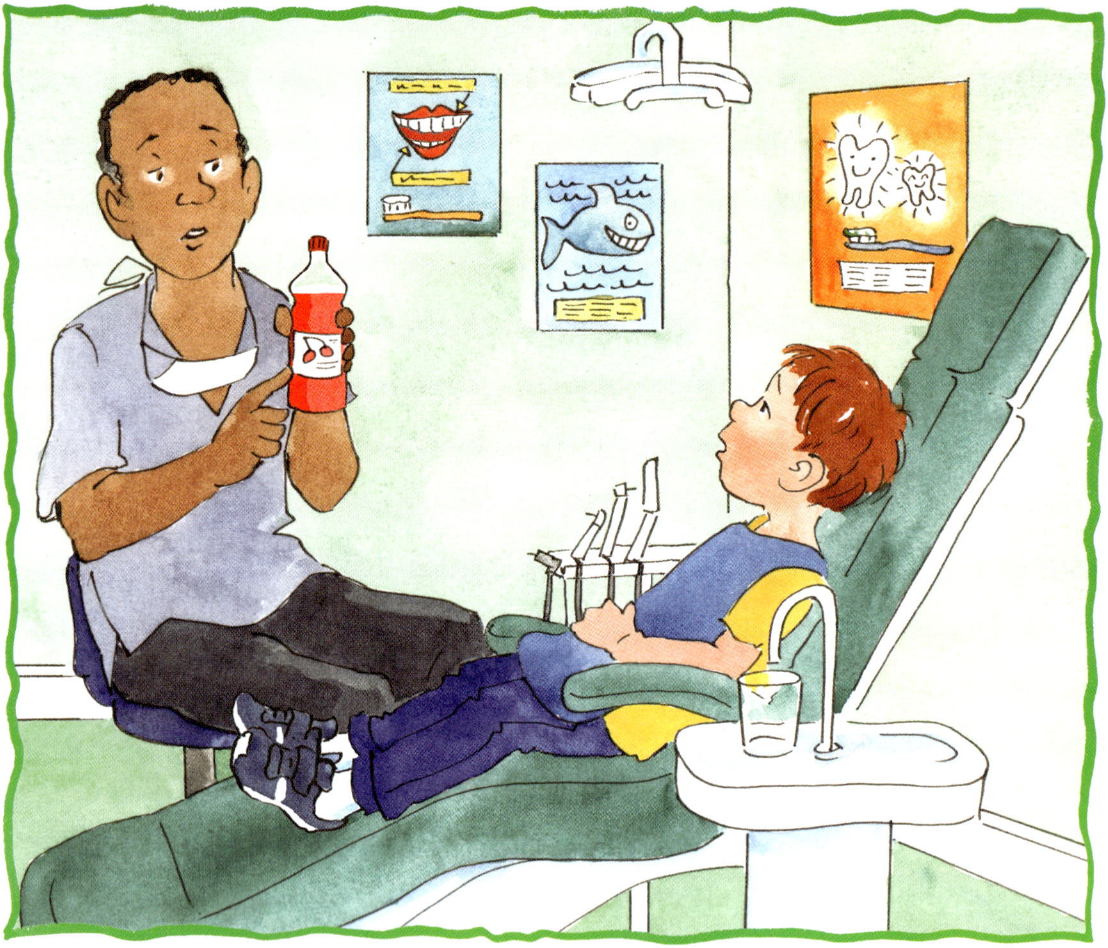

Jack has lots of sweets and fizzy drinks in the holidays, and doesn't take time to brush his teeth. Now his teeth are hurting. The dentist tells Jack he has a cavity and needs a filling. He advises him to have fewer sugary foods and drinks.

Why does Jack need a filling?

Healthy Teeth

Jack switches to water or milk and has low-sugar snacks, such as cheese and crackers. The next time Jack visits the dentist he gets a sticker for trying so hard and remembering to clean his teeth twice a day.

What can you choose instead of sugary drinks?

Eating Processed Foods

Sabina reads the box her dinner came in and she doesn't know what many of the ingredients are. She sees too that it contains added salt and sugar. Her mum explains that they are added in the factory. **Why should we not eat too many processed foods?**

Eating Fresh Foods

Sabina and her mum grow peas, herbs and strawberries on their balcony and some cress on the windowsill. These foods are easy to grow and so tasty to eat, and now Sabina knows what she is eating. **What could you grow in your outside space?**

I can grow food to eat

Not Involved in Cooking

Harry usually watches TV while his dad cooks. He often doesn't like the look of his dinner because he doesn't know what's in it. His dad suggests that he helps to choose and cook their meals.

Why doesn't Harry know what he is eating?

Helping in the Kitchen

Harry didn't realise how many ingredients went into his meals and how much fun it is to plan and cook them. He peels vegetables, stirs in herbs and really enjoys eating what he has created.
How could you help with cooking dinner?

Glossary

Balanced diet – the right foods in the right amounts to give your body all the nutrients it needs

Calcium – a micronutrient found in dairy foods and dairy-free alternatives that helps build strong bones and teeth

Dairy foods – foods that are made from milk, such as cheese or yogurt

Iron – a micronutrient found in many protein foods that helps your body to make blood

Lactose – a type of sugar found in milk products

Nutrient – a substance that our bodies need to survive, such as water, carbohydrates, fats and proteins

Micronutrient – a substance needed in very small amounts, such as vitamins and minerals

Nutrition – everything about food and how it is used by our bodies

Protein foods – foods that help your body to grow and repair itself

Processed foods – foods that have been made and packaged in a factory. Extra ingredients or processes are often used to make them last longer

Starchy foods – foods that provide energy

Encourage your child to use the picture stickers and answer the questions in the book.